Jellyfish

by **David C. King**

mc **Marshall Cavendish**
Benchmark
New York

Series consultant
Paul Sieswerda
New York Aquarium

Marshall Cavendish Benchmark
99 White Plains Road
Tarrytown, NY 10591-9001
www.marshallcavendish.us

Library of Congress Cataloging-in-Publication Data

King, David C.
Jellyfish / by David C. King.
p. cm. — (Animals, animals)
Summary: "Describes the physical characteristics, behavior, and habitat of jellyfish"—Provided by publisher.
Includes bibliographical references and index.
ISBN 0-7614-1867-9
1. Jellyfishes—Juvenile literature. I. Title. II. Series.

QL377.S4K573 2004
593.5'3—dc22
2004021441

Photo research by Joan Meisel

Cover photo: John Henry Williams/Bruce Coleman, Inc.

The photographs in this book are used by permission and through the courtesy of: *Bruce Coleman, Inc.:* Jane Burton, 11;
Carlos Villoch, 16; Dale Kneupfer, 27. *Corbis:* Stephen Frink, 4, 32; Kevin R. Morris, 42. *Peter Arnold, Inc.:* Sea Studios,
Inc., 6; Fred Bavendam, 12; Kelvin Aitken, 18, 20, 36, 41; Reinhard Dirscherl/Bilderberg, 21; Manfred Kage, 24; F.
Pacorel, 28; A. & J. Visage, 30; Roland Birke, 34; Norbert Wu, 38. *Photo Researchers, Inc.:* Gregory Ochocki, 1, 13;
Gregory G. Dimijian, MD, 9; Mark Harmel, 14; Andrew J. Martinez, 15 (top); A. N. T., 15 (bottom); Phanie, 23.

Series design by Adam Mietlowski

Printed in China

1 3 5 6 4 2

Contents

1 Introducing Jellyfish 5

2 Jellyfish Defenses 19

3 A Jellyfish Day 25

4 The Life of a Jellyfish 33

5 Jellyfish and People 37

Glossary 44

Find Out More 46

Index 48

1 Introducing Jellyfish

When we see a jellyfish floating near the shoreline or washed up on the beach, it looks like a lifeless, colorless blob. But what seems to be a blob is really one of nature's most fascinating creatures. Jellyfish are found in all of the world's oceans, and they can be divided into more than two hundred species, or kinds, of jellyfish.

Jellyfish are one of the earth's oldest creatures. They have been floating in the world's oceans for about 650 million years. That means they were here before the dinosaurs.

A jellyfish, of course, is not made of jelly, and it isn't a fish. So what kind of animal is it? It has no head, no eyes or ears, no feet or legs, no brain or heart, and no bones.

A jellyfish is not a fish. The two creatures may share the same underwater world, but they are quite different from each other.

A bell jelly shows off its mass of tentacles.

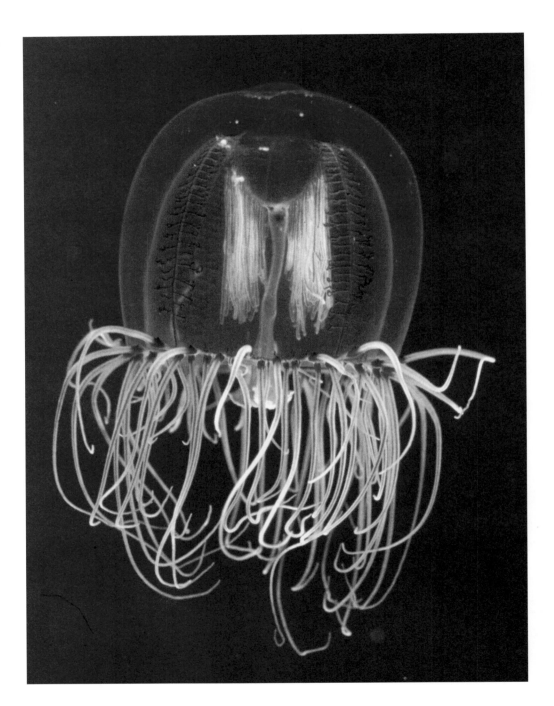

Jellyfish are *invertebrates*—animals without a skeleton. They are made up of a body with arms and *tentacles* hanging underneath it. Jellyfish come in an amazing variety of shapes and sizes. The most common body form is called a *medusa* and is shaped like a bell or umbrella. In some species, the medusa is less than 1 inch (2.5 centimeters) across. In others, such as the North Atlantic lion's mane, the body can measure 8 feet (2.5 meters) across.

The arms and tentacles that hang down from the body also show great variety. In some species, the tentacles are only a few inches long. In others, the tentacles reach much farther than that. The tentacles of the Portuguese man-of-war, for example, can grow to be 165 feet (50 meters). On a baseball diamond, they would stretch from home plate to first base and more than halfway to second.

Jellyfish also look and act in a variety of ways. The upside-down jellyfish does not float in the water. Instead, it anchors itself to the ocean floor, with its short arms and tentacles reaching up, rather than hanging down. It looks more like a bowl of plants than a jellyfish.

The Jellyfish

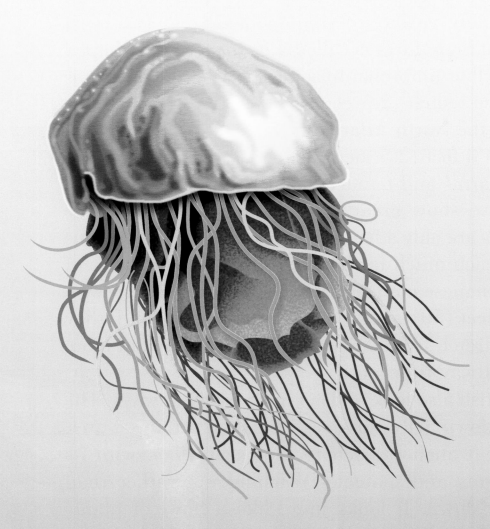

Made mostly of water, jellyfish do not have skeletons and lack the common body organs—such as a heart or a brain—that most animals possess.

A close-up look at the Portuguese man-of-war's long tentacles.

The bodies of jellyfish appear to be fragile—and they are. One reason is that about 95 percent of their bodies is water. You can look into this almost *transparent* shape and see the jellyfish's organs. They usually display a range of colors, including orange, pink, blue, purple, and deep violet.

Jellyfish are usually seen in shallow coastal water, but they can be found in almost every part of the ocean. Scientists have even discovered a few species living at depths of nearly 30,000 feet (9,000 meters). And, while most species prefer warm waters, some are comfortable in frigid subarctic temperatures.

When you see jellyfish floating in the ocean, they appear to be motionless. But if you could look on the underside of the body, you would see that the arms and tentacles are busy, either capturing tiny fish or guiding the prey to the jellyfish's mouth. The muscles around the rim of the body can *contract*, or tighten. This motion is similar to letting the air out of a balloon; the escaping air pushes the balloon forward. This ability is especially useful for vertical, or up-and-down, movement. If the sun has made the water too warm, for example, the jellyfish can move into deeper, cooler water.

The medusa body is round and *symmetrical.* This allows the jellyfish to respond to signals about food or danger from any direction. No matter where the signals are coming from, they take the same amount of time to reach the control center. That control center is not a brain, but a simple nervous system called a *nerve net.*

A jellyfish may appear to be still in the water, but the arms and tentacles are constantly moving.

Species Chart

Lion's Mane
This small jellyfish measures 8 inches (20 centimeters) or less across the bell, or medusa. It has reddish brown arms and eight clusters of tentacles. It is also known as the winter jelly because it appears in coastal waters during the colder months.

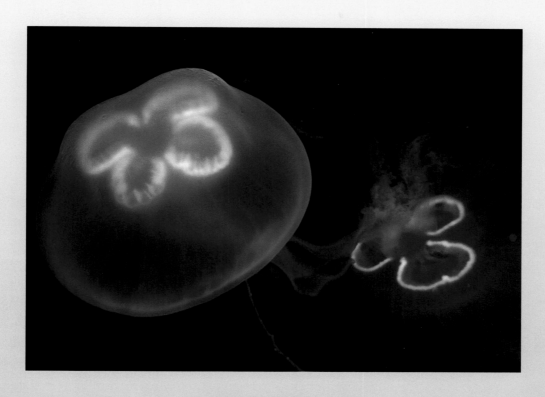

Moon Jelly

Like the lion's mane, the moon jelly's medusa
is saucer shaped. It is also semi-transparent,
revealing four horseshoe-shaped organs. The
moon jelly's body can measure from 8 to 20
inches (20 to 51 centimeteres) in diameter.

Species Chart

Sea Nettle

Sea nettles are about 6 to 8 inches (15 to 20 centimeters) in diameter. They are one of the great nuisances on American beaches because they often float close to shore or wash onto the sand. Oral arms and tentacles hang from the medusa, which is red or brown and saucer shaped. The sea nettle's sting is mild, but it can come as an unpleasant surprise to a swimmer.

Upside-Down Jelly

The upside-down jelly is often seen in the shallow waters of Florida's mangrove swamps. Anchored to the seabed, with its frilly tentacles reaching upward, it looks something like a bowl of blue-green lettuce or cauliflower. The body is usually about 12 inches (29 centimeters) wide.

Portuguese Man-of-War

Beneath the man-of-war's body the often curly tentacles can reach lengths of 165 feet (50 meters). The man-of-war's sting is very painful to humans, producing shock, fever, and difficulty breathing.

Special cells in the nerve net called receptors can detect important information, such as changes in light or in water temperature. The jellyfish can then take whatever action is needed.

By expanding then quickly contracting, a jellyfish can move itself away from the sun's heat.

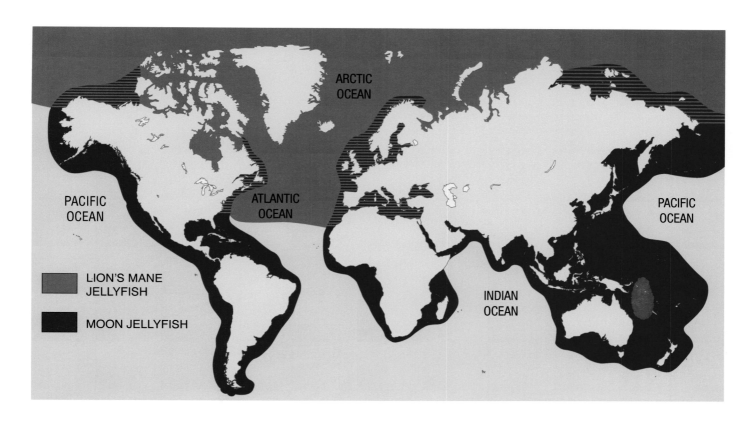

ARCTIC
OCEAN

PACIFIC
OCEAN

ATLANTIC
OCEAN

PACIFIC
OCEAN

LION'S MANE
JELLYFISH

MOON JELLYFISH

INDIAN
OCEAN

A jellyfish's digestive system is even simpler than its nervous system. A single opening serves as the mouth. It takes in food and also gets rid of waste. Between four and eight arms are located near the mouth. They draw in the food that has been captured by the tentacles.

Jellyfish are found in all of the world's oceans. This map shows the range of two common species.

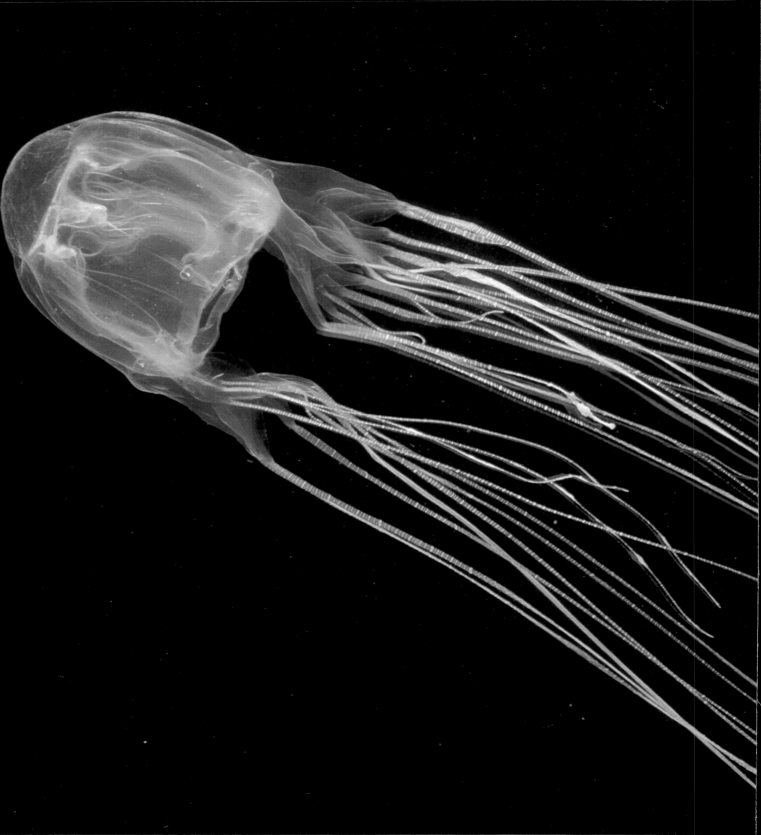

2 Jellyfish Defenses

Jellyfish do not have many ways of defending themselves, but what they do have works quite well. They need good defenses because there is little they can do to get away from *predators*. The Australian sea wasp, also called the box jellyfish, is thought to be the fastest-swimming jellyfish. By rapidly expanding then contracting its bell-shaped body, it thrusts itself forward. But, at top speed, the sea wasp is lucky to reach 5 miles (8 kilometers) per hour. At that rate, it would not escape most predators, such as a large fish or an osprey.

The main defense for most jellyfish are its special stinging cells, called *nematocysts.* These cells are buried in the jellyfish's tentacles and look like tiny *barbed*

The box jellyfish cannot move fast, but its toxins are deadly. Humans have died within four minutes of being stung.

darts. When an intruder, such as an attacking fish or a loggerhead turtle, touches the tentacles, the contact triggers the release of thousands of stinging cells. These cells act like tiny harpoons being shot into the predator. The nematocysts release a toxin, or poison, that instantly stuns or paralyzes the creature. The toxin of some species, such as the Portuguese man-of-war and the Australian sea wasp, can be quite powerful and extremely harmful to humans.

The defense systems of the larger jellyfish include a tangled grouping of arms and tentacles. The North

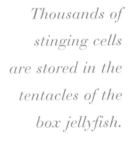

Thousands of stinging cells are stored in the tentacles of the box jellyfish.

Atlantic lion's mane jellyfish has forty to sixty tentacles stretching down 100 feet (30.5 meters) or more. Far below the animal's body, these tentacles form a network, like a giant spiderweb. Any fish or turtle that accidentally swims into the net is instantly harpooned by the stinging cells. As the intruder thrashes about, trying to escape, the motion simply triggers more darts.

This kind of defense system serves several purposes. It not only protects jellyfish, it also helps them to gather food. In addition, the presence of these pain-causing stinging cells in some species serves as a warning that benefits all types of jellyfish. Many bird species avoid all jellyfish, for example, because they cannot tell which ones have stinging cells and which do not. So, even perfectly harmless jellyfish receive some protection from those that have toxin-filled darts in their tentacles.

The appearance of jellyfish also helps to defend them from predators. These almost transparent blobs simply do not look very *appetizing*. Nevertheless, seagulls and other birds will sometimes peck away at a large jellyfish, hoping to reach one of the colorful organs within. Sometimes they succeed. However, since water makes up more than 95 percent of the jellyfish, the bird usually gives up before it reaches anything it could actually eat.

The large number of dangling tentacles also helps to prevent attack. A fish trying to swallow a jellyfish often ends up with a mouthful of forty or fifty tentacles. Birds of prey find it difficult to try to carry off such an odd-shaped creature as well.

The fact that most jellyfish are almost colorless is still another form of defense. As many swimmers have reported, jellies are so transparent that you find yourself looking right through them. At best, only a faint outline is seen. This semi-transparency is a form of *camoflauge* that helps protect the jellyfish from predators.

Many species of jelly-fish are so transparent they are hard to see. This is one more form of defense.

3 A Jellyfish Day

One of the many unusual things about jellyfish is that, in spite of their helpless appearance, they are predators. They hunt other animals. But, unlike most predators, they cannot actively pursue their prey. Since they do not move any faster than the sea wasp's 5 miles (8 kilometers) per hour, it is unlikely they would catch many fish.

Instead of chasing its prey, the jellyfish waits for it. Smaller jellyfish feed on tiny sea creatures called *plankton.* Plankton are found in all bodies of water and are made up of many species of plants and animals. Some are so small a microscope is needed in order to see them. Other, larger plankton include green algae and tiny shellfish. Most kinds of plankton cannot swim but drift instead on the ocean currents. The patient jellyfish simply waits for its meal to come floating by.

This is what some kinds of plankton look like when seen under a microscope.

With little effort, the arms of the jellyfish scoop the plankton into its mouth. In an almost constant action, the jellyfish is able to graze on the endless selection of plankton.

In some species of small jellyfish, the tentacles are quite short, forming a kind of fringe around the edge of the body. The tentacles beat rapidly, pulling water and plankton toward the sticky arms. The arms then scoop the food into the mouth where the plankton is scraped off the arm and swallowed.

For large jellyfish, feeding themselves is a bit harder. The jellyfish must wait for a fish to accidentally swim into its tangle of arms and tentacles. Depending on the size of the jellyfish, there may be anywhere from ten to sixty tentacles, each reaching from 45 feet (15 meters) to three times that length.

As soon as a fish or any other sea creature brushes against the tentacles, the dart-like stinging cells release their toxin. The prey is either stunned or killed. At the same time, the arms of the jellyfish start to coil, bringing the food up to the mouth, where it is swallowed and digested. These arms are located around the mouth and scientists refer to them as *oral arms*.

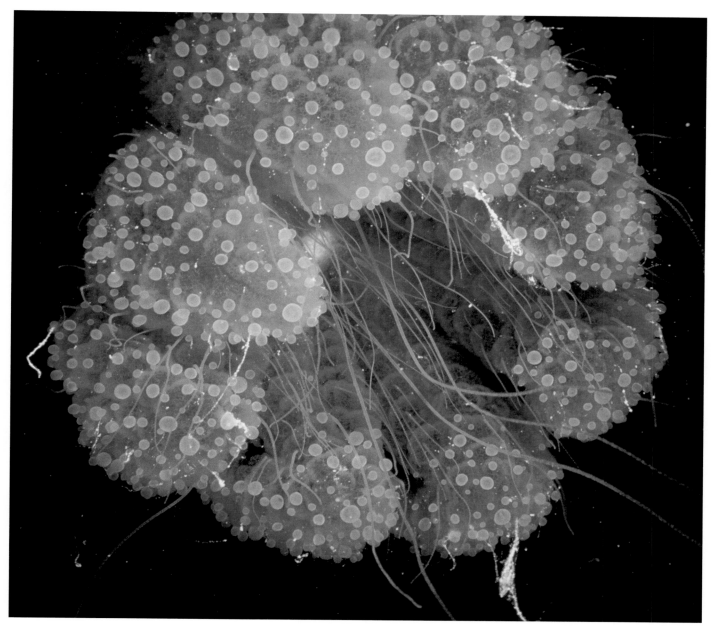

In smaller jellyfish that have short tentacles, the arms are in constant motion, pulling plankton toward the mouth.

Some fish seek out the company of jellyfish for protection.

One tiny species of fish, known only by its scientific name of *Nomeus*, lives among the tentacles of the Portuguese man-of-war without being stung. It is one of the few creatures unharmed by the toxin contained in the stinging cells. This bold little fish survives by biting off small pieces of the tentacles. The jellyfish does not resist because the missing pieces of tentacle easily grow back. The only drawback to this arrangement is that sometimes the man-of-war eats the little fish by accident.

Gathering food is quite different for the upside-down jellyfish. Living in the shallow coastal waters of Florida and the islands of the Caribbean, the upside-down jelly is anchored to the sea floor with its short arms and tentacles reaching up. Like the common jellyfish, an upside-down one picks tiny food particles out of the water that is constantly floating through its frilly network of tentacles.

The upside-down jellyfish also gets energy another way—from sunlight. Algae living on the arms of the jellyfish act like green plants, turning sunlight into food through the process called *photosynthesis*.

Like most sea creatures, jellyfish spend nearly all of their time gathering food. As they do this, they drift

While jellyfish usually float in the water alone, some cluster together.

wherever the currents, tide, or waves carry them. Most jellyfish are loners, but sometimes they are found floating in large groups. In the Gulf Stream of the North Atlantic, for example, Portuguese men-of-war are occasionally seen by the thousands, forming one huge group that stretches for several miles.

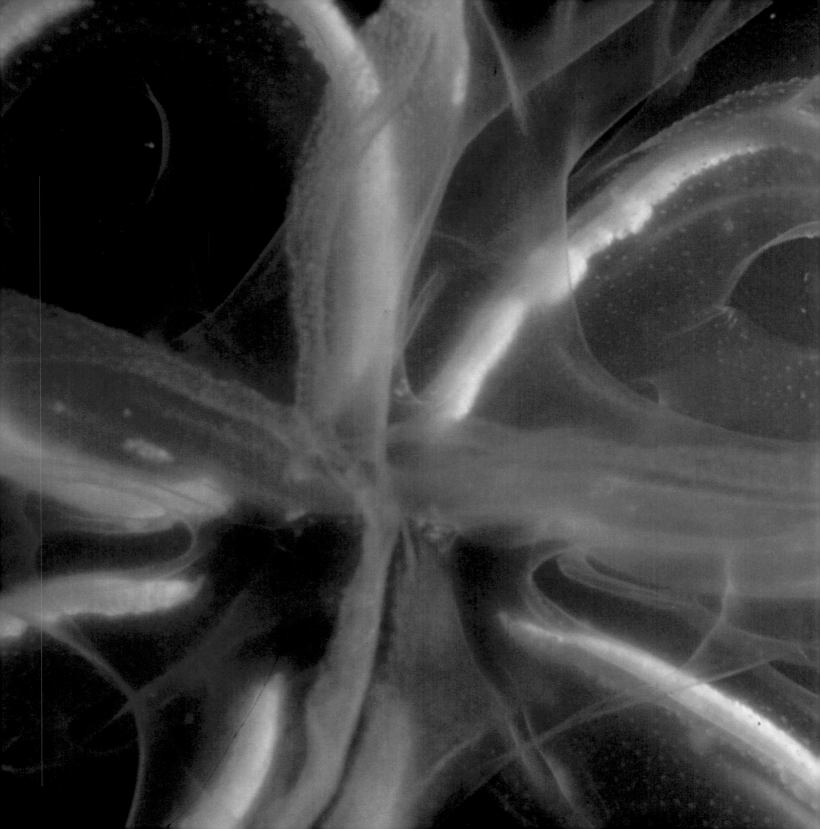

4 The Life of a Jellyfish

Jellyfish go through two separate and very different life stages. The most common stage is when the jelly is in its medusa form, when the body is shaped like a bell or an umbrella. Most of the jellyfish we see in the world's oceans are in this stage.

The jellyfish's first and other main life stage begins at birth. Then, newborn jellies are in the *polyp* form, and the jellyfish is anchored to the ocean floor. The newly hatched *larva* is flat, with small tentacles around the edge of its body. These tentacles act like tiny paddles, helping to move the jelly away from its parent. After a few days, the future jellyfish sinks slowly to the sea floor. A stalk grows from its body and

From these coiled organs, the moon jellyfish releases its eggs into the water.

attaches to anything solid on the seabed. The short tentacles then start to grow and catch food.

As the polyp gets bigger, the top half splits from the bottom, producing a second polyp. More divisions occur in a process called *budding*. Each newly created polyp then floats away and grows into an adult in the medusa form.

As the polyp stage begins, the larva is round and flat.

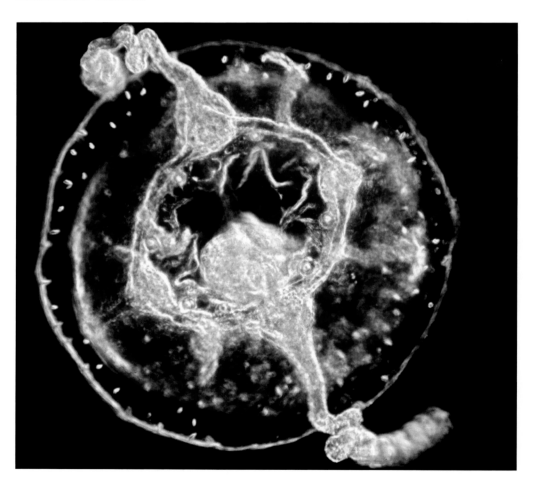

It is believed that a jellyfish can live for up to five years in the polyp stage. In the more familiar medusa stage, jellyfish live only a few months, although some species may live for up to two years.

In the medusa stage, there are both male and female jellyfish. Several times per year, most species gather in large numbers to increase the chances of fertilizing the eggs produced by the female. The female releases the eggs into the water and lets them float away. In some species, like the common jellyfish, the eggs stick to the female's arms until they hatch.

Jellyfish and People

Most jellyfish are harmless to humans. The sting of some species can be mildly painful, while the toxin produced by a few can be extremely painful. Far worse, the most poisonous species have been known to cause death in humans.

The deadliest of all species is the Australian box jelly. Its toxin is said to be more powerful than the venom of the cobra, one of the world's deadliest snakes. The box jelly, also known as the sea wasp, is big. Its body can be as large as a soccer ball and the tentacles, numbering forty or more, can be more than 15 feet (4.6 meters) long. The tentacles are so transparent they are almost invisible, and of course they contain countless nematocysts.

A beach sign in Australia warns bathers to watch out for box jellyfish.

A diver's suit offers protection from a jellyfish's stinging cells.

Swimmers in the coastal waters of Australia learn to be cautious about the sea wasp. Jellyfish do not attack humans, but trouble can occur if a swimmer comes in contact with the web of tentacles. The thousands of stinging cells are triggered, and they stab into the victim. The struggle to break free simply makes the problem worse. The sting causes severe pain, like an electric shock. This is followed by an upset stomach, vomiting, and difficulty breathing. The victim can die within a few minutes.

Scientists have found that certain kinds of covering over the skin can prevent the release of the stinging cells. Australian lifeguards discovered that women's panty hose provide perfect protection. Many of them now wear panty hose on their arms and legs when they are out on a rescue. To the lifeguards, safety is more important than how they look. Protective suits are also available, and some substances, such as vinegar, help to reduce or soothe the sting.

The sting of the Portuguese man-of-war, like that of the sea wasp, is extremely painful to humans and can result in death. Signs are often posted on beaches when large groups of men-of-war have been sighted. The signs often include warnings not to touch any of the jellies that may wash up on shore and to stay away from pieces of the tentacles.

Many species of jellyfish release a much milder toxin designed to stun their prey. In humans, this can cause mild pain or merely a stinging sensation. The sting of the sea nettle is quite painful to people, for example, but milder pain or tingling is felt from the sting of the moon jelly.

The moon jelly is one of the most common jellyfish found in the waters of the Caribbean and Mediterranean seas. Hundreds at a time are sometimes washed on shore after a storm. In some Mediterranean countries, young boys play a game in which they hurl beached moon jellies at one another until the boys' bodies, arms, and legs tingle from multiple stings.

Apart from any danger, many species of jellyfish are simply a nuisance or a bother to humans. Sometimes entire groups of jellyfish wash ashore, making beaches unsafe. Even if the jellies are harmless, the smell of decaying jellyfish can be quite strong. Jellyfish can also pose a problem for the crews of fishing boats, especially when masses of them become tangled in fishing nets. The crews find that cleaning the clogged nets is almost impossible.

The crest, or top part, of the Portuguese man-of-war reminded people of the sails on a once common ship called a man-of-war.

A fisherman lands a large jellyfish with his net.

While most people find nothing at all useful about jellyfish, in some cultures certain species are considered a delicacy, or a rare treat. In several Asian countries, for example, mushroom jellies are eaten either plain or pickled.

Even if you never taste a jellyfish, you can appreciate these amazing creatures for their variety of sizes and shapes. Their graceful and often colorful appearance in the water also helps to set them apart. It is no wonder that the jellyfish has now become one of the most popular attractions at public aquariums. An aquarium is the perfect place to learn more about these unique creatures, as there you can see them in their underwater world with no chance of being stung.

Glossary

appetizing: Good or pleasing to eat.

barbed: Having a sharp, often pointed edge.

budding: The process in which jellyfish polyps divide.

camoflauge: A means of hiding or concealing.

contract: To tighten or clench.

invertebrate: An animal without a backbone or skeleton.

larva: A stage of development for certain living things after they have hatched from an egg.

medusa: The common body shape of jellyfish, like a bell or umbrella.

nematocysts: Stinging cells.

nerve net: The cluster of cells called receptors that act like a simple brain, picking up signals and forming the needed response.

oral arms: The parts of a jellyfish that are clustered around the mouth opening.

photosynthesis: The process of turning the sun's energy into food.

plankton: Tiny plant and animal life found floating in bodies of water.

polyp: The early stage of the jellyfish life cycle when it is anchored to the seabed and reproduces by budding.

predator: An animal that hunts other animals for food.

symmetrical: Having identical halves or sections.

tentacles: The long, flexible parts of the jellyfish that usually hang down from the body and are used to catch food.

transparent: Clear, allowing light to pass through.

Find Out More

Books

Dornhoffer, Mary K. *Jellyfish.* Mankato, MN: Compass Point, 2003.

Gowell, Elizabeth Tayntor. *Sea Jellies: Rainbows in the Sea.*
Danbury, CT: Franklin Watts, 1993.

Landau, Elaine. *Jellyfish.* Danbury, CT: Children's Press, 1999.

Sharth, Sharon. *Sea Jellies: From Corals to Jellyfish.* Danbury, CT:
Franklin Watts, 2002.

Taylor, Leighton. *Jellyfish.* Minneapolis: Lerner, 1998.

Web Sites

Swimmers Beware: Jellyfish Are Everywhere
http://www.nationalgeographic.com/ngkids/9608/jellyfish/

Jellyfish Links
http://cybersleuth-kids.com/sleuth/Science/
Marine_Life/_Jellyfish/

Freshwater Jellyfish!
http://nsm1.nsm.iup.edu/tpeard/JELLYFISH.HTML

Vancouver Aquarium Marine Science Center
http://www.vanaqua.org/education/aquafacts/jellyfish.html

Public Aquariums

The New England Aquarium
Central Wharf
Boston, MA 02110
(617)973-5200
www.neaq.com

The Maritime Aquarium
10 North Water Street
Norwalk, CT 06854
(203)852-0700
www.maritimeaquarium.org

The Florida Aquarium
71 Channelside Drive
Tampa, FL 33602
(813)273-4020
www.flaquarium.net

National Aquarium in Baltimore
Pier 3, 501 E. Pratt Street
Baltimore, MD 21202
(410)576-3800
www.aqua.org

Monterey Bay Aquarium
886 Cannery Row
Monterey, CA 93940
(408)648-4876
www.mbayaq.org

Oregon Coast Aquarium
2820 SE Ferry Slip Road
Newport, OR 97365
(541)867-3474
www.aquarium.org

Index

Page numbers for illustrations are in **boldface**.

algae, 25, 29
aquariums, 43, 47
arms, 7, 10, **11**, 17, 20, 26, 29, 35
    See also oral arms

beach, 5, 14, 40
birds, 21, 22
budding, 34

digestive system, 17, 26

fish, **4**, 5, 10, 19, 20, 21, 22, 26, **28**, 29
food, 10, 22, 25–30

invertebrates, 7

jellyfish
    box, **18**, 19, 37
        See also sea wasp
    lion's mane, 7, 12, **12**, 17, 20–21

jellyfish
    moon, 13, **13**, 17, 40
    Portuguese man-of-war, 7, 15, **15**, 20, 29, 31, 39, **41**
    Red Sea crown, **21**
    sea nettle, 14, **14**, 40
    sea wasp, **18**, 19, 20, 25, 37, 39 *See also* box jellyfish
    upside-down, 7, 15, **15**, 29

larva, 33
life span, 35
life stages, 33–35

map, 17
medusa, 7, 10, 12, 14, 33, 34, 35
mouth, 10, 17, 26

nematocysts, 19, 20, 37
nerve net, 10, 16

oral arms, 14, 26
organs, 5, 8, 9, 13, 22

photosynthesis, 29
plankton, **24**, 25, 26
polyp, 33–35, **34**
predators, 19, 22, 23, 25

receptors, 16

skeleton, 7, 8
species chart, 12–15
stinging, 14, 15, 19–22, 26, 29, 37, 39–40

tentacles, **6**, 7, **9**, 10, **11**, 12, 14, 15, 17, 19, 20, **20**, 21, 22, 26, **27**, 29, 33, 34, 37, 39
toxin, 20, 22, 26, 29, 37, 40

About the Author

David C. King is an award-winning author who has written more than forty books for children and young adults. He and his wife, Sharon, live in the Berkshires at the junction of New York, Massachusetts, and Connecticut. Their travels have taken them through most of the United States.